The
Quotable
FARM
ANIMAL

MBI

First published in 2005 by MBI, an imprint of MBI Publishing Company, Galtier Plaza, Suite 200, 380 Jackson Street, St. Paul, MN 55101-3885 USA

MBI titles are also available at discounts in bulk quantity for industrial or sales-promotional use. For details write to Special Sales Manager at MBI Publishing Company, Galtier Plaza, Suite 200, 380 Jackson Street, St. Paul, MN 55101-3885 USA.

All photographs by Norvia Behling except for page 10, which is by Shirley Fernandez.

ISBN-13: 978-0-7603-2338-0
ISBN-10: 0-7603-2338-0

Editor: Amy Glaser
Designer: Mandy Iverson

Printed in China

You can milk a cow

the **wrong way** *once*

and still be a farmer,

but vote the wrong way

on a water tower

and you can be in *trouble*.

John F. Kennedy

Animals are such agreeable *friends*—

they ask no questions, they pass no criticisms.

✦

George Eliot

Spring is nature's way

of saying,

"Let's party!"

Robin Williams

Animals often strike us as *passionate machines*.

＊I＊

Eric Hoffer

Don't count your

chickens *before* they

are hatched.

✦

Aesop

The mere brute *pleasure* of reading—

the sort of *pleasure* a COW must have in grazing.

—✦—

Lord Chesterfield

She always says, my lord,

that *facts are like cows.*

If you look them

in the face hard enough

they generally run away.

✢

Dorothy L. Sayers

Most sorts of *diversion* in men, children, and other animals

are in imitation of *fighting*.

—I—

Jonathan Swift

Don't brood:

you're a *human being*, not a *hen*.

❦

Anonymous

The best thing about **animals** is that *they don't talk much.*

·‖·

Thornton Wilder

An animal's *eyes*

have the power

to speak a **great language**.

—⊦—

Martin Buber

It's true that I did get the girl,

but then my grandfather always said,

even a blind chicken finds a few grains of corn

now and then.

＋

Lyle Lovett

The love

for *all* living creatures

is the *noblest* attribute

of man.

—⬩—

Charles Darwin

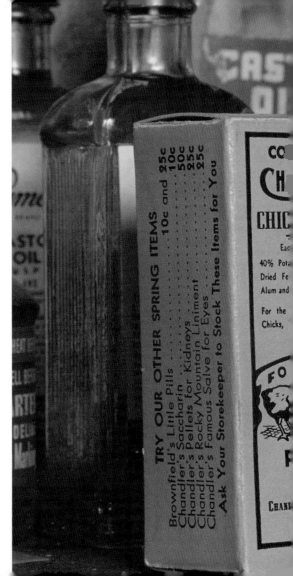

I actually would love to live in New York.

But I need land; I need space.

I'd love to move to a place

where *I could have a lot of land and a goat.*

—I—

Lusia Strus

If **happiness** truly consisted

in *physical ease*

and *freedom from care*,

the happiest individual

would not be either a man

or a woman;

but an **American** cow.

❖

William Lyon Phelps

When one tugs at

a *single thing* in **nature**,

he finds it **attached**

to *the rest of the world.*

⊷⊶

John Muir

Once you have *heard* the lark,

known the swish of feet through hilltop grass,

and *smelt* the earth made ready for the seed,

you *are never again going to be fully happy*

about the *cities* and *towns*

that man carries

like a crippling weight upon his back.

—⊣⊢—

Gwyn Thomas

If we didn't live *venturously*,

plucking the wild goat by the beard,

and **trembling** over precipices,

we should *never be depressed*,

I've no doubt;

but already *should be faded*,

fatalistic, **and** aged.

—◦—

Virginia Woolf

If it's **true** that **men**

are such *beasts*,

this must account for the fact

that most **women**

are *animal lovers*.

⊶⊷

Doris Day

Regard it as *just as desirable* to build a **chicken house**

as to build a **cathedral**.

—I—

Frank Lloyd Wright

I go to nature to be soothed and healed,

and to have *my senses put in order.*

‹†›

John Burroughs

The cow is *nothing but a machine* which makes grass fit for us *people to eat.*

❧

John McNulty

Look at those cows

and remember

that the *greatest scientists*

in the world

have **never discovered**

how to make grass into milk.

Michael Pupin

I go on *working* for the same reason

that a hen does on *laying eggs.*

—✦—

H. L. Mencken

Put a *silk* on a goat and it is *still a goat*.

—◦I◦—

Irish Proverb

Just living is not enough . . .

One *must have* sunshine,

freedom, and a little flower.

―❖―

Hans Christian Anderson

The cow is of the *bovine ilk*;

one end is **moo**, the other **milk**.

✦—✦

Ogden Nash

If I didn't start **painting**, *I would have raised chickens.*

⊹

Grandma Moses

That the *sky is brighter than the earth*

itself is appreciated and enjoyed.

Its beauty loved gives the right to aspire

to the *radiance* of the sunrise and the stars.

—I—

Helen Keller

Forget not that *the earth delights* to feel your bare feet

and the winds long to *play* with your hair.

✦

Kahlil Gibran

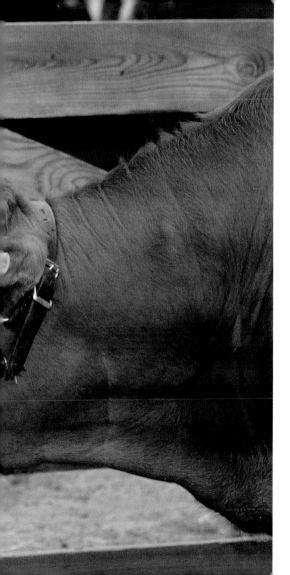

The *quality of life*

is *determined* by its activities.

⊷I⊷

Aristotle

I love that *quiet time* when nobody's up

and the **animals** are *all happy to see me*.

—+—

Olivia Newton-John

If you've broken the eggs,

you should make the omelette.

❖

Anthony Eden

The key to everything is patience.

You get the chicken *by hatching the egg*, not by smashing it.

⊷

Arnold G. Glasow

A **cow** is a very good animal *in the field*;

but *we turn her out of a garden*.

＊I＊

Samuel Johnson

It is a **rule** of nature

that *taking a day off*

on a farm

sets a person back

at least a week.

⊷⊶

Jane Hamilton

Ironically, **rural America**

has become viewed

by a growing number

of Americans

as having a higher

quality of life

not because of *what it has,*

but rather because of

what it does not *have!*

◦-I-◦

Don A. Dillman

Business is never so healthy as when,

like a chicken,

it must do a certain amount of

scratching around for what it gets.

—I—

Henry Ford

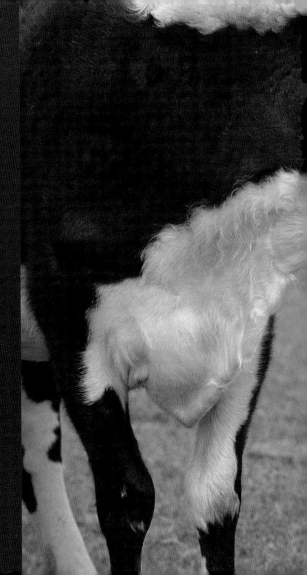

Cows are amongst the *gentlest*

of breathing creatures;

none show more *passionate*

tenderness to their young

when deprived of them;

and, in short,

I am not ashamed to profess

a deep love for

these *quiet creatures*.

⁘

Thomas DeQuincey

Don't approach a *goat* from the **front**,

a *horse* from the **back**,

or a *fool* from **any** side.

✦⬩✦

Yiddish Proverb

Have you ever noticed

that a rooster runs with his hands in his pockets?

✦╪✦

Lucien Guitry

The only Maybelline I knew

was the *name of a cow.*

—⊹—

Chuck Berry

Heaven is *under our feet* as well as *over our heads.*

✦

Henry David Thoreau

Don't put **all** your *eggs* in **one** basket,

unless you're at the supermarket.

⊷

Anonymous

When a cow *laughs*, does milk come out her nose?

＋Ｉ＋

Anonymous

ABOUT THE PHOTOGRAPHERS

Norvia Behling's photographs have appeared thousands of times in books, magazines, and calendars. She has been capturing the unique qualities of her subjects for 25 years. She divides her time between her farm in Wisconsin in the summers and her home in Florida in the winters. Norvia is married with one daughter.

Shirley Fernandez has been handling animals and fluffing fur for 15 years. She has been grooming, cleaning, and holding the animals for photographer Norvia Behling who encouraged Shirley to try her hand behind the camera. Shirley lives in Sarasota, Florida with her husband, 2 horses, 2 dogs, 10 cats, 7 chickens and many other assorted critters, and still manages to drive a school bus and meet once a week with the 4-H dog club.